NORTHFIELD BRANCH
847-446-5990

SESAME STREET

COME TOGETHER, CHANGE THE WORLD

A Sesame Street Guide to Standing Up for Racial Justice

Jackie Golusky

Lerner Publications ◆ Minneapolis

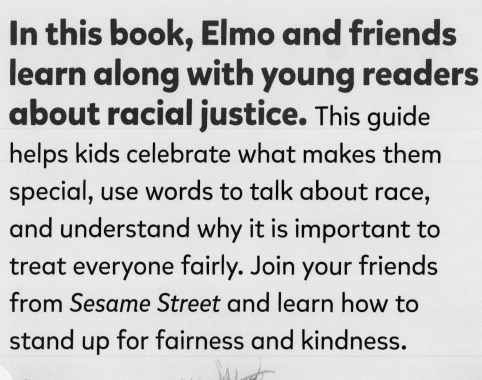

In this book, Elmo and friends learn along with young readers about racial justice. This guide helps kids celebrate what makes them special, use words to talk about race, and understand why it is important to treat everyone fairly. Join your friends from *Sesame Street* and learn how to stand up for fairness and kindness.

TABLE OF CONTENTS

LEARNING TOGETHER

Lots of people live on Sesame Street. **Everyone is special.**

Let's celebrate our diversity and learn about racial kindness and fairness.

Elmo wants to learn with you!

Everyone has a skin color. It is part of what makes us unique.

All skin colors are beautiful.

My beautiful skin is a part of who I am!

Some people don't think all skin colors are beautiful. Sometimes, people are not treated fairly or kindly because of their skin color, hair texture, eye shape, or what language they speak.

I want everyone to feel loved on Sesame Street!

Being treated unfairly because of your race or where you are from is called racism. Racism has been around for a long time, and it's made a lot of things unfair.

We can work together to make today and tomorrow better.

We can stand up together for racial kindness and fairness.
This is called racial justice.

13

We have differences. We have a lot in common too.
We all like to have fun with friends.

Elmo, Rosita, and I are good friends. We love story time!

UPSTANDING IS OUTSTANDING

We can speak up when we are treated unfairly or when our friends are. **That's what being an upstander means.**

How can you be an upstander?

Do Your Part!
Talk with a trusted adult about being an upstander. You can ask questions you have about racial justice.

As upstanders, we listen with our ears and our hearts to those who have been treated unfairly.

When we see someone being treated unfairly, we act. Tell a grown-up what happened. Then help the friend who was hurt.

Sometimes that means sitting quietly with them.

If you have been treated unfairly or your feelings are hurt, tell someone who cares about you. It could be a parent, a teacher, or a friend.

I like to talk to my mom.

Do Your Part and Draw What's in Your Heart!
Show and share feelings that may be too big for words.

Let's come together and treat people fairly.

Everyone is welcome to grow and share their food at our community garden.

We're better together.
We help make the world a kinder
place for all when we treat
everyone fairly and kindly.

Be an Upstander!

We are playing with friends, but they won't let someone play because of that person's skin color. What could we do?

Tell an adult.

Tell our friends that's not fair.

Listen to the person.

Invite the person to play.

Play a new game with the person.

29

GLOSSARY

racial justice: treating all races, ethnicities, and cultures with respect

racism: treating people unfairly because of their skin color, eye shape, hair texture, language, or where they are from

unique: being the only one of its kind

upstander: someone who stands up when they or their friends are treated unfairly

LEARN MORE

Easton, Emily. *Enough! 20 Protesters Who Changed America.* New York: Crown Books for Young Readers, 2018.

Madison, Megan, and Jessica Ralli. *Our Skin: A First Conversation about Race.* New York: Penguin, 2021.

Miller, Marie-Therese. *Caring with Bert and Ernie: A Book about Empathy.* Minneapolis: Lerner Publications, 2021.

INDEX

PHOTO ACKNOWLEDGMENTS

Ariel Skelley/Getty Images, pp. 4, 6, 24 (right); kali9/Getty Images, pp. 5, 11, 17, 22, 26; DanielBendjy/Getty Images, p. 7; Richard T. Nowitz/The Image Bank/Getty Images, p. 8; GagliardiPhotography/Shutterstock.com, p. 9; FatCamera/Getty Images, p. 12; LightField Studios, p. 14; Tom Williams/CQ Roll Call via AP Images, p. 16; weedezign/Shutterstock.com, p. 18; Jose Luis Pelaez Inc/Getty Images, p. 20; SDI Productions/Getty Images, p. 21; TwilightShow/Getty Images, p. 23; John P Kelly/Getty Images, p. 24 (left); Jupiterimages/Getty Images, p. 25.

Lerner Publications Company
An imprint of Lerner Publishing Group, Inc.
241 First Avenue North
Minneapolis, MN 55401 USA

For reading levels and more information, look up this title at www.lernerbooks.com.

Main body text set in Mikado. Typeface provided by HVD.

Editor: Rebecca Higgins **Designer:** Laura Otto Rinne
Photo Editor: Cynthia Zemlicka **Lerner team:** Martha Kranes

Library of Congress Cataloging-in-Publication Data

Names: Golusky, Jackie, 1996– author.
Title: Come together, change the world : a Sesame Street guide to standing up for racial justice / Jackie Golusky.
Description: Minneapolis : Lerner Publications , [2022] | Includes bibliographical references and index. | Audience: Ages 4–8 | Audience: Grades K–1 | Summary: "Elmo and friends learn along with young readers about racial justice. This gentle guide informs kids what it means to stand up for justice and what they can do in their daily lives"– Provided by publisher.
Identifiers: LCCN 2021000074 (print) | LCCN 2021000075 (ebook) | ISBN 9781728429014 (library binding) | ISBN 9781728431437 (paperback) | ISBN 9781728429021 (ebook)
Subjects: LCSH: Racial justice—Juvenile literature. | Sesame Street (Television program)—Juvenile literature.
Classification: LCC HM671 .G638 2022 (print) | LCC HM671 (ebook) | DDC 323—dc23
LC record available at https://lccn.loc.gov/2021000074
LC ebook record available at https://lccn.loc.gov/2021000075

Manufactured in the United States of America
1-49414-49509-4/9/2021